Text copyright © 1974 by Educreative Systems, Inc. Illustrations copyright © 1974 by Creative Education. International copyrights reserved in all countries. No part of this book may be reproduced in any form without written permission from the publisher. Printed in the United States. Library of Congress Number: 73-10289   ISBN: O-87191-261-9

Published by Creative Education, Mankato, Minnesota 56001
Prepared for the Publisher by Educreative Systems, Inc.
Distributed by Childrens Press, 1224 West Van Buren Street, Chicago, Illinois 60607

Library of Congress Cataloging in Publication Data
Zalewski, Ted.
    Vince Lombardi—he is still with us.
    SUMMARY: A brief biography of the football coach who turned Wisconsin's Green Bay Packers into a virtually unbeatable team.
    1. Lombardi, Vince—Juvenile literature.
[1. Lombardi, Vince. 2. Football—Biography] I. Title. GV939.L6Z34 796.33'2'0924 [B] [92]
73-10289 ISBN 0-87191-261-9

ViNCE
LOMBARdi
HE IS STILL WITH US

by Ted Zalewski

Illustrated By John Nelson

"Winning isn't everything. It's the only Thing."

Vince Lombardi

Could the Green Bay Packers win the National Football League Championship three years in a row? The Dallas Cowboys were trying to stop them. It was December 31, 1967 in Green Bay, Wisconsin.

The Dallas Cowboys were ahead 17 to 14. Time was running out. Thousands of fans kept looking up at the clock. Only 4 minutes and 50 seconds to go.

Many of the fans looked toward the Packer bench. A short man was walking up and down the sideline. He waved his arms back and forth. He growled at his players as if he were a bear who had just lost his honey. He seemed to be shouting, "Get going now! You can do it! You're the Packers." He was the coach. His name was Vince Lombardi.

It's cold in Green Bay - 13 degrees below zero. The players move around, trying to get warm. Fifty thousand fans are in the stands. They are all wearing heavy coats, hats and earmuffs. Many of them have blankets wrapped around their shoulders. The clock is ticking away.

Out on the field, Starr throws a pass to Anderson. It's good for 9 yards. The Packers are now on the Dallas 30 yard line. Two minutes are left to play. The Cowboys dig in. They are determined to stop the Packers.

In the huddle Bart Starr calls for a pass. The players line up on the line of scrimmage. Starr gets the ball and runs backward a few yards. He throws a pass to Mercein. The play is good for 19 yards! The Pack is on the 11 yard line. The Packers are closing in!

Bart Starr hands off to Anderson. He bangs to the one yard line. Anderson tries two more times to go over the goal line. He can't do it. The Cowboys are holding the line.

Starr calls a timeout. There are only 20 seconds left to play. He jogs over to the sideline. Lombardi tells him what to do.

Starr returns to the huddle. He looks at Jerry Kramer, the right guard and says, "Darn it, I want it in there, nothing short of the goal. It's up to you, Kramer!"

The ball is snapped. Kramer smashes into Pugh. Pugh is knocked backwards. Starr puts his head down and runs behind Kramer. Starr falls down over the goal line. A touch-down! The Packers win! There are only 13 seconds left on the clock. Fans run all over the field.

After the game the Packers fought their way through wild fans. Together the men said the Lord's Prayer. Then they shouted and jumped around. They were the Champions once again.

The T.V. men rushed into the locker room. Many of them surrounded Jerry Kramer, the right guard. He was the man who had blocked for the touch-down.

"There's a great deal of love for one another on this club .... Many things have been said about Coach, and he is not always understood by them who quote him. The players understand. This is one beautiful man."

Vincent Thomas Lombardi was born in New York City on June 11, 1913. He was the first son of Henry and Matilda Lombardi. Vincent's father had come from Italy and settled in Brooklyn, New York. Vincent's mother was born in America.

Vince grew up in an Italian-American family. His father's job was to earn money and be the head of the family. Mrs. Lombardi's job was to care for the house and the children. As Vince was the oldest in his family, Mr. Lombardi told Vince what to do. Then Vince told his brothers and sisters what to do. It was an Italian custom.

Mr. Henry Lombardi was a butcher. He had only gone to the sixth grade in school. Yet he read many books and spoke two languages. He expected much of his three sons, Vince, Harold and Joe. He wanted them to get as far as possible.

Vince picked up a fiery temper from his father. Later in life when Vince was a coach, men weighing 280 pounds would shake when he got angry. Yet, like his father, he would listen to the problems of his players. He made them feel proud of themselves.

As a boy Vince wanted to be a priest. Every Sunday he would go to Mass. The priest would ask the people to do the best they could. Vince respected

priests more than any other people in the world. Yet, he didn't think he could handle the job. But he never forgot his dream. All his life he had priests for friends.

Vince turned to football. He wasn't a natural athlete, and he wasn't very big. Neither was he a fast runner. Yet Vince wanted to be a winner more than anything else.

Vince tried hard! He became a star fullback at St. Francis Prep School. He loved to run across the line of scrimmage, squeezing the ball in his hand, heading for the goal line. He was good—good enough so that Fordham University in New York offered him a scholarship.

Lombardi had to work hard. He didn't even play first string in his second year at Fordham. He weighed 185 pounds and was 5 feet 8 inches tall. As a guard he played against men weighing 210 to 220 pounds. He learned to block them. He learned to throw his body at their knees. A teammate of Vince, Alex Wojciechowicz, said, "He was ready to kill himself to win." The line Vince played for became known as the Seven Blocks of Granite.

The Seven Blocks of Granite were hard, tough ball players. Few teams could push them aside. Some say they were the greatest college line of all time.

Vince had a hard time accepting defeat. In the last game of his college career, Fordham was to play New York University. Fordham had not lost a game all year. It was a close game. But New York won 7-6. Vince took the defeat hard. For several days, he wouldn't even talk.

After college Vince had a hard time finding a job. He was too small to play pro football. The country was still in the depression. So Vince entered Fordham Law School. After two years of law he quit because he planned to marry. Now he would have to get a job.

He finally found one as a teacher and coach at St. Cecilia High School in Englewood, New Jersey. It was an important job for him. Now he was making the change from player to coach. And he loved his work. He and his wife Marie felt close to each other. They were working together to get ahead.

Lombardi was a tough high school coach. His younger brother, Joe, went to St. Cecilia's when Vince was a coach there. Joe remembers that time well, "At St. Cecilia, we didn't have a blocking sled for the football team. We had to hit Vin instead. Every guy on the club had to do it every day, and I was always the first to hit him and the last."

Lombardi always tried to get his players mentally ready for the game. Once St. Cecilia was to play a game against Brooklyn Prep. It would be a tough game. Vince got all his players together in the locker room. He gave everyone a pill. He said the pill would make every player bigger. All the players believed him. St. Cecilia went out on the field and won 6-0. The pills were made of sugar.

In 1947 Lombardi got a chance to move up as a coach. He was in his thirties and knew that he wanted to be a full-time coach. When a job opened up at

Fordham University, he applied for it. But after two years at Fordham, Vince was ready to move ahead.

The next step for Vince was the most important one in his coaching career. He became an assistant to Colonel Black at West Point in 1949. At that time the Colonel was one of the finest coaches in America.

Vince had much to learn as a coach. He still needed to learn to control his temper. Colonel Black tells a story about Vince on the first day of practice

in 1949. "I remember that day. He was standing near me, talking about a minor detail on the practice schedule. Suddenly somebody in his group, one of the linemen, did something wrong. The linemen were probably seventy-five feet away, and he dashed over there, screaming at the top of his lungs. I yelled, 'Vince,

Vince,' and he pulled up short, like a charging horse. He was explosive. Of course, he was still immature. That was really his only shortcoming when he first joined us."

Five years later, it was time for Lombardi to leave. He felt close to Colonel Black. Years later when he was at Green Bay he would call the Colonel as much as once a week to ask his advice.

In 1954, Lombardi became the assistant coach for the offense of the New York Giants. He began immediately to build a strong offense. Few men liked him at first. To them he was just a high school and college coach. What did he know about the pros?

Vince made a special point to know his players. He'd visit his men in their rooms in the evening. He ate with them when they had games on the road. Soon the men began to like him. They teased Vince by hiding his baseball cap.

He was rough on his men. Vince showed the men movies of their mistakes. He got angry—so angry that he sometimes smashed the projector. Many of the players also got angry. They said they would punch him in the face at the end of the season. Yet it never happened. The players respected him.

Alex Webster, a tough fullback with the Giants, said of Vince: "He was a hard man, but you had to respect him. He knew what he was doing, and he proved it to us. I think he made all of us twice the players we might have been."

In 1959 Vince was worried. He had been an assistant coach for many years. He was waiting for the chance to have his own team. The Green Bay Packers were in trouble. They had had many years as a losing team. In 1958 their record was 1 win, 10 losses, and 1 tie. Some thought they were the worst team in football. Lombardi was offered the Head Coaching job. He accepted.

On January 28, 1959 Vince Lombardi signed a five year contract with the Green Bay Packers. He

was 45 years old. The contract gave him complete control over the team.

Vince met with reporters on that day. He said the following:

"This is the moment I have been waiting for all my life. I will put winning above all else here. Winning is gained through discipline. I've never been with a losing team before in my life, and I don't intend to start now!"

Vince took over immediately. When the Packers showed up at training camp in 1959, they met a coach who meant business. From morning until night they did push-ups, sit-ups and jumping jacks. They ran and ran and ran. Vince screamed at them. He yelled so much that he lost his voice at the end of the first week of practice. He was like a man gone crazy.

As coach he took Paul Hornung off the bench and made him into a halfback. He changed Ray Nitschke into a middle linebacker. Some men he praised. He treated others like dogs. He made his men work hard. They were to become some of the greatest football players of all time.

The Packers came back! In their first year under Vince, Green Bay won 7 games and lost 5. Teams grew to fear the Packers.

In 1961 Vince put together one of the greatest teams in all of football history. Some experts thought they were as strong as the 1941 Chicago Bears. The Pack was like a tank that couldn't be stopped. That year they beat Baltimore 45-7. They smashed Cleveland 49-7. They bulldozed San Francisco 30-10. Twelve Packers made the national all-pro team. They won the Western Conference Championship with a record of 11 wins and three losses. They then faced the Giants for the National Football League title. Would Vince remember his old team? If he did remember them kindly it didn't make him slow down the Packers. They won 37-0!

Year after year the Packers won. In nine years
they won 98 games, lost 30 and tied 4. They won 5
National Football League Championships and two
Superbowls. The little city of Green Bay became known
as *Titletown, U.S.A.* It still was not enough for Vince.

He said, "We never won as many as I wanted, which was all of them."

His players grew to love him. He was like a father to many of them. He told them: "Only three things should matter to you: Your religion, your family, and the Green Bay Packers. In that order."

Fuzzy Thurston, all pro-tackle, said of him, "He didn't push; he led."

Bart Starr, all-pro quarterback, said, "I owe my life to that man."

In 1967 the Packers beat the Oakland Raiders 33-14 in the second Superbowl. The Packers were on top of the football world. Yet Vince was tired and worn out. For nine years he had worked day in and day out. And he had given his all.

Not too long after winning the Superbowl, he left the game he loved. Vince left coaching.

At first he was happy. No longer did he worry about game plans. No longer did he worry about broken legs and bad knees. No longer would he yell and scream at men. He would be able to rest.

Then July 15 came. It was the first day of Packer practice. Vince had made plans to play golf that day. Then he decided not to. He decided to go to practice. He stood on the sidelines, watching the football players practice. He saw his players do jumping jacks, "one two, one two, one two," and he felt like a bear who couldn't growl. He turned his eyes away from the field. It hurt inside of him. He knew then that he should never have left football.

He missed players asking him, "Coach, I need some help because my baby's sick." And when his "kids" Paul Hornung or Boyd Dowler were doing well, he was proud of them. Vince knew he would have to go back to football.

In the winter of 1969 Lombardi became the head coach of the Washington Redskins. The Redskins had not had a winning season since 1955. Vince said it was more challenging to build something than to keep it going. So he started again.

He made friends with Sonny Jurgensen, the quarterback. Even though the men were very different, they respected each other. He asked Sam Huff to come out of retirement. Sam said, "The only reason I came back to football was to be able to be with him." By the end of the first year, the Redskins had a record of 7 wins, 5 losses and 2 ties. Vince had brought home another winner.

"You never lose. But sometimes the clock runs out on you."

Vince Lombardi

It was early in the summer of 1970. Vincent looked forward to another year at Washington. He wanted to build another powerful team, like the Packers.

Then, in mid-June, he felt pains in his stomach. They would go away and then come back again. The pain got worse. After many tests, the doctor ordered him into the Georgetown Hospital.

On June 27, Vince underwent surgery. It seemed to go well. Everything would be all right. He returned home. He told a friend, "I'll beat this, I'm gonna beat this thing."

Vince didn't get better. On July 27, he had a second operation. This time the news was bad. He had cancer. It was a deadly cancer, one that would take his life no matter what the doctors did.

The Redskins heard the news. They didn't know what to do. One player, a defensive tackle, was so upset he left camp. The players walked around with their heads down. They thought of Vince lying in a hospital bed. He was dying.

Soon the bad news had travelled across the United States. Vince Lombardi didn't have much longer to live. His old friends came from everywhere to see him. Willie Davis, former all-pro defensive end of the Pack, flew in from Los Angeles. He saw Vince for only two minutes. Willie said, "I had to go, I had to. That man made me feel important."

Jerry Kramer was close to Vince. He visited the coach. Jerry remembered well what was said:

"It's good to see you, Coach. I've been worrying about you. I've been praying for you. My mom asked me to tell you she's praying for you, too."

Vince lay very still. "Jerry, I'm just so tired. I just can't talk to anybody - not till I get this thing licked."

Early in the morning on September 3, 1970, Vince Lombardi, the Coach, died.

Sonny Jurgensen said of Vince: "I still feel he's with us all the time."

3 Indy Wins

CREATIVE'S
SUPERSTARS

Mark Spitz   Billie Jean King
Jackie Robinson   Vince Lombardi
Johnny Bench   Roberto Clemente
Wilt Chamberlain   Jack Nicklaus
Joe Namath   Jerry West
A. J. Foyt   Bobby Hull
Arnold Palmer   Muhammad Ali
Bill Russell   O. J. Simpson
Tom Seaver   Hank Aaron